MASTER GUIDE TO STRESS

HOW TO SURVIVE IN A WORLD FULL OF CHAOS

JESSICA BORUSHOK, PH.D.

YOUR PSYCHOLOGY

CONTENTS

INTRODUCTION

For years I have been on the hunt for low-cost resources for my clients to supplement the work we do in session.

I was frustrated with the misinformation, overly complicated or complex explanations, and just poorly produced products. Finally, after publishing my first book, that I wrote for therapists, I decided to stop waiting for someone to create the resources I needed and to create them myself.

This book is part of that process. It is the first in a series of brief guides to deal with some of life's common yet tricky issues.

I created Busy Mind Reboot (www.busymindreboot.com) to provide a platform for my ebook series, online courses, audio books, guided meditations, worksheets, and more.

Master Guide to Stress is the first book in this series because frankly stress is a universal problem. Common solutions to stress fall along the "get over it," "push through," "it could be so much worse" continuum. And while in the moment pep talks can help us navigate hurdles it's not exactly a long-term approach to living.

Rather, I have included the science-backed practical information without the fluff or unnecessary historical descriptions to give you only the information that you need to have a better relationship with stress and take control of your life.

Your time is valuable and I respect that.

Before moving on to the first part of this book I'd like you to consider whether you are ready to tackle stress at this moment in your life. I mean it. If buying this book is another strategy to help you feel that you are doing something, yet you know you will never put any of the strategies into practice please do not buy this book.

If it will fall onto a stack of other unread self-help books use the money you'd put toward this book to buy yourself a nice cup of hot chocolate or download a song you love from iTunes.

It is way more important to me that you are devoting your time, energy, and money toward something that is meaningful to you. If this book is not that I understand and appreciate the honesty.

But if it is, if you're ready and willing to not only read but live and practice what is outlined in these chapters then I can promise it will take you closer to what matters most to you.

In this book, you will learn how to understand the way stress and our desire to avoid stress impacts how we live. You will answer questions that help you formulate an idea in your mind about the type of life you want to live and what moving towards that life looks like. You will identify strategies for taking back your time, sleeping better, and finding peace even in chaos.

You will have all the tools to overcome overwhelm, get unstuck, take back your precious time and put it to good use toward the people and things that matter most to you.

Happy Reading!

———

Quick Disclaimer: The case examples described in this book do not represent real clients or actual people, but rather are used for demonstration purposes to highlight the common ways these strategies can have an impact on a person's life.

This book is designed to serve as a self-help resource and is not a substitute for mental health services. If you are in crisis or are experiencing significant distress that is impacting your life, please consider seeking help from a mental health professional.

Resources such as Psychology Today or the "find an ACT therapist" tab on contextualscience.org are a good place to start. Your medical doctor may also have recommendations for professionals in your area.

Seeking professional help can be an important step toward improvement for many people. Therapy is not reserved for only those with severe or significant impairments. Some choose to seek professional help before issues get to that point and it's definitely something to consider.

1

THE TICKING TIME BOMB

YOU'VE HEARD IT BEFORE, from friends, your family, your partner—stress is going to kill you one day if you don't start taking care of yourself.

One day you'll just drop dead.

Poof!

While the dramatics make it easy to shrug off, thinking to yourself that as soon as you get through this one promotion, or this big move, or this huge life transition you'll slow down, take a break, the truth is that they aren't wrong.

Chronic stress is a ticking time bomb.

The problem is that stress, like food, is helpful in any normal situation; it gives you a boost to run around after your kids or grandkids, it helps you keep it all together while you juggle a million little tasks, makes you focused during a big presentation at work, and pulls you through that extra shift.

But just like food, too much and it starts to wear down your system, making you less efficient, less focused, less healthy. A chocolate chip cookie for dessert once per week? Delicious. Eaten every day and you begin to feel sluggish, the pounds start to creep up, and your doctor lectures you (even more) on the importance of diet and exercise.

For some reason though, we have a tendency to downplay the impact stress has on us. We blame a poor night of sleep, a project at work, or a conflict at home, but we don't stop to connect the dots and realize that this moment of stress has been going on for a lot of moments now.

Maybe we are afraid that if we stop moving and examine our stress it will finally overpower us. Maybe we are so out of tune with our bodies that our symptoms of stress are out of our awareness. Maybe we just don't want to know.

This book is for people who are finally ready to look at their stress and do something about it. Because whether we acknowledge it or not, it's there, and it's wreaking havoc in our lives and our bodies. The strategies in this book work, but only if we are willing to look at stress head on and face some hard truths.

In case you aren't convinced of the impact stress can have on our lives, here's a list of some of the unfortunately real outcomes that persistent, chronic stress leads to. If you'd like to take a deep dive into the science of how stress impacts our bodies, minds, and emotions I'd recommend reading *Why Zebras Don't Get Ulcers* by Robert Sapolsky:

Performance:

poor memory

trouble concentrating

Stress sucks the life out of our drive and focus.

Emotions:

depressed mood

anxiety disorders

irritability and anger

Stress wears us down.

Functioning:

chronic muscle tension

sleeplessness

decreased arousal

digestive symptoms

Stress interrupts the normal rhythm of our bodies.

Health:

poor immune system

diabetes

high blood pressure

stroke

heart attacks

Stress makes it more likely we'll have an adverse medical condition.

So I guess it is true, you can drop dead from stress. The problem is it takes so long before we notice the impact. Stress is something that compounds year after year, just like that daily chocolate chip cookie: from one day to the next we don't notice any difference, but from one year to the next? Or ten? And the impact is astounding.

If you find yourself experiencing one of the above symptoms, or just feel stuck in a spinning wheel that's going nowhere, then it may be time to pause and notice what's going on in your life, and if what you are doing to manage stress is helping or hurting.

In an effort to control our stress we tend to do things that help in the moment, such as eat a whole bag of chips, skip the gym for a nap, drink alcohol, smoke a cigarette, do drugs, yell at a partner, binge-watch Netflix, or avoid completing tasks altogether because we're just too overwhelmed and can't deal right now.

Or maybe you do the opposite: you throw yourself into your work trying to drive away that feeling of being behind and making that voice in your head that says, *I'll never be caught up, never be good enough*, go away for a little while only for it to return even stronger later.

These short-term fixes feel good in the moment, that's why we keep doing them even when we have serious talks with ourselves about the problem with binge-watching Netflix.

It works for a little while.

But it's just that: **a temporary solution to a long-term problem.** And in our efforts to stop smoking, exercise more, and work harder we miss the fact that these behaviors aren't the cause of our stress; **they are a byproduct**, what happens as a result of continued stress. In order to tackle chronic stress, we need a longer-term outlook.

In the spirit of looking to the future, ask yourself these questions.

What do you do to try to make the stress go away?

My go-to is ordering in pizza for dinner and eating half the box. My friend works 14 hour days and never allows herself a moment to pause. When stress shows up in your life, what do you do to minimize or eliminate the experience?

Does it work in the short term?

For me it does, stuffing myself on pizza always makes me feel better right away—it just doesn't last too long.

And you? I'm willing to bet that your attempts to move away from stress provide some relief in the short-term.

If you find yourself saying, "No WAY!" slow down to that moment right when you make the decision to do whatever it is you do to cope. Is there a moment of relief, a delicious moment of escape, before the thoughts come in to judge or the guilt or anxiety sets in?

Generally, I've found that any behavior we do regardless of whether we or others label them as "good" or "bad" continue because they provide some type of reinforcement, even if it is only a temporary relief.

Does it work in the long-term?

Eh, I find myself unable to fit into my favorite jeans, I'm less social because I just don't have the energy or desire to be around others, I'm hard on myself as I don't like how I look, and my mind keeps throwing out more and more thoughts criticizing my body and later myself in general.

As a result, I'm more distracted at work, my friends are

asking me where I've been, and the stress I was so desperately trying to avoid comes back tenfold.

What about you? Do the actions you do to cope with stress work in the long term to get you where you want to be in life? Do they permanently eliminate stress? After the moment passes are you better off or back to square one? If I were a betting person—I'm not, but still—I'd wager that your answers are no. Maybe even a big, emphatic NO!

Whether out in the world or in our heads we generally have one go-to strategy. It may show itself in different forms, but at the end of the day, it is the same: attempt to avoid, escape, control stress.

And when it doesn't work, instead of pausing and wondering if our approach is the problem, if our overall idea of what we need to do to move forward and move on actually works, we decide we must not be trying hard enough or maybe we just don't have the right tool. And we double down (and beat up ourselves).

Why do we keep doing the same things over and over again?

Have you ever heard the quote, "the definition of insanity is doing the same thing over and over again, but expecting different results"? I'd say that's being human, not insane.

For some reason, unlike any other animal species on the planet, if something doesn't work we just keep on doing it. Every other animal tries something else.

A mouse wandering through a maze looking for the way out (and the cheese) may first try the obvious way, but after reaching a dead end you'd see them backtrack and try different routes eventually finding success.

A human in a maze?

They'd come to the dead end and decide with single-minded focus that this is the only way forward and would begin to push through the thick bramble full of thorns and rough branches, picking up cuts and scrapes along the way, only to reach the other side, celebrate, and find themselves against a new dead end to push through.

We, the all-intelligent humans, try to control and eliminate stress, and when it doesn't work for the long haul we keep trying to make it go away no matter how many experiences we have that that approach does not work.

Why is that?

Humans have the gift and curse of language, of thought. When we face a problem we can't solve or an emotion we can't eliminate our minds tell us, "*you're not trying hard enough*," "*other people aren't stressed*," "*they're better than you*," "*you'll never make it*," "*you're pathetic*." And those thoughts, those emotions, hurt.

I know I certainly don't like hearing my mind tell me what a failure I am, or how I'll never be on par with everyone else.

So we work hard to make those thoughts and feelings go away, we try to convince ourselves it isn't true by challenging our thoughts: "*I can do this, I am hardworking and a good* _____ [parent, employee, student, partner, person], *I will succeed.*"

We try to avoid thoughts and feelings through binge eating, drinking in excess, fighting with people we care about, working insane hours every day, spending all of our waking hours in our heads overthinking every move and planning out every potential pitfall looking for a way out; we try to control our minds.

The only problem is that IT DOES NOT WORK.

Let me say that again: trying to permanently control or eliminate our thoughts and feelings Does. Not. Work.

Often the more we struggle to make a thought, feeling, memory or physical sensation go away, the stronger and louder it gets.

That's a scientific fact, not my personal musings.

Sometimes what we're fighting against comes back with friends (worry about worry, anger at sadness, guilt over stress, fear of a pounding heart). Don't believe me? That's okay.

I want you to doubt me. I want you to take time for yourself to really think about what your experience of stress has been. Think of how hard you have worked to try to manage stress. How many different approaches have you tried? How much time have you sacrificed? Honestly, has it gotten better?

Think back to when this stress first appeared, is it smaller or larger now?

Is stress the only thing that shows up or do other feelings or thoughts pop up alongside it?

Let your experiences show you what you've suspected for a while: **you can't control stress**, you can't avoid stress, you can't make it go away, not without significant cost and even then it's only temporary.

The problem with this is that while we're spinning in circles trying to avoid the unpleasant stuff that shows up, we're missing out on all the things that actually matter to us. Unless of course, that's just me.

Really pause and notice—what are you missing out on that matters to you?

If you're like me, then you forget sometimes what you're working towards in the first place and why it even matters. Why you want to better manage stress. What our attempts to control stress have gotten in the way of.

I forget sometimes, that the reason I work so hard is so I can have a long life doing what I love; so I can connect with the people who are important to me, and make a difference in the world. I forget that I love the outdoors: the way the sun feels against my skin after a cold, long winter, and the warmth that spreads through my body during a hike among the trees or a rollerblade listening to my favorite music. I forget that my job is important to me not only because it helps me achieve the above things, but also because it fosters my curiosity and feeds my love of learning and allows me to help others.

What do you forget?

I want to be clear that I am not saying, suck it up, get over it, just accept that stress is a part of life. That's incredibly invalidating and frankly not helpful at all. And I truly do not believe that.

There are behaviors that can help you cope with high-stress moments, bring your mind into focus, better manage your time, improve the quality of your interactions, increase your energy, and help you connect with the life you want to create for yourself—we'll get to that in the coming chapters

—but none of that work is relevant if we're trapped in a cycle of avoiding, dulling, controlling stress and all the thoughts, feelings, sensations, and memories that come along with it; that come along with life really.

Now it may seem crazy to put a pause to these patterns, you may think "*what are you talking about? That's the only thing keeping me afloat right now.*"

But if you've answered those earlier questions honestly, then you know from your own experiences that this pattern of reacting isn't working—it's like closing our eyes, covering our ears, and singing a happy tune; the stress bomb is still ticking even if you pretend it's not there.

So again, I ask you to take a moment and notice. Notice whether your actions are taking you closer to what matters to you, or whether you're simply closing your eyes, covering your ears, and singing your happily ever after while experiencing none of it.

Putting practice into action—write down the answers to the following questions:

1. Who and what matter most to you? What qualities or characteristics do you want to be about? We call these our values.

2. What stressful thoughts, feelings, memories, or physical sensations show up that get in the way of moving towards the people and things in question one?

3. What do you do either that others can see you do (observable behaviors) or mental strategies you use (planning, overthinking, worrying, etc.) to try to control, manage, avoid, or

escape the stressful thoughts, feelings, memories, or physical sensations you wrote down in question two?

4. If you weren't focused on trying to control or escape your stressful thoughts, feelings, memories, and physical sensations what would I see you doing (get specific!) that would take you a step closer to who and what matter to you and the type of qualities or characteristics you want to possess?

Are you willing to let go of your control strategies, try something new, and come into contact with stress if it means you can move toward what matters to you?

2

MINDFULNESS FOR THOSE WHO
AREN'T MINDFUL

I WAS SITTING in a workshop during the beginning of a mindfulness exercise, the ringing vibration of a singing bowl reverberating in the air, and suddenly I wanted to laugh thinking of my client earlier that week talking about how he wasn't interested in "*that hippie shit.*"

I've heard many versions of that phrase before, harkening back to the image of mindfulness as meditation that requires nimble legs to fold themselves into a seated pretzel, gentle hands that kiss their fingertips together, an empty mind, and the sound of '*om*' light on the breath.

It's in this image that so many people reject the modern idea of mindfulness—a practice centered around the focus on and awareness of the present moment—despite the incredible scientific backing of its practice. Research has shown that even as little as twenty minutes a day for seven weeks can have a significant impact on brain development.

You read that right, mindfulness practice, this practice of noticing, can lead to organic changes in the grey matter of the brain, particularly in the prefrontal cortex responsible for executive functioning: planning, organizing, completing tasks, as well as changes in the amygdala, helping people better regulate their emotions so they can find themselves in that stable place where they can experience their emotions without being sucked in. Instead of inside the chaos of an emotional tornado.

Functions that anyone and everyone would be envious of.

So you don't like sitting still and clearing your mind? That makes two of us.

In fact, the mere idea of it makes me either very tired or extremely on edge. I promise you that's not my aim.

My goal for you is to improve clarity around the thoughts, feelings, and sensations that show up for you. To provide a choice of how you want to act when that stuff shows up— when the stress creeps in and tries to hijack your body—all in the service of increased focus on activities that are impor- tant to you, whether that is a work deadline, a conversation with a loved one, or a blissful ten minutes of downtime when you do pause.

Or in other words, better performance in all aspects of your life.

Like any muscle in our body, we can train our minds to do certain tasks. However, when our minds run on autopilot, they tend to spend little time in the present moment, unless in the face of an imminent threat.

Rather, our minds focus their attention on tearing apart every detail of past mistakes to find out what went wrong to prevent similar future mistakes or creating alternative realities where your life unravels differently or imagining uncertain futures in order to prepare for potential problems.

And frankly, this is adaptive.

Our minds act as threat detection systems, hyper-focused on our survival, not our happiness. When we are in safe environments, and in today's society, statistically speaking, we are relatively safer than in the past, it makes sense that our minds would spend time and energy to address potential future threats and understand past threats.

What about you? Does your mind tend to focus more on past mistakes or future problems, or perhaps the proverbial "*what if*"?

The problem with automatically drawing your attention outside of the now is that the mind could go forever creating monsters from shadows, winding your body up as it throws every potential obstacle in your way, and diverting your attention from your actual life—you know, the one you're living right now.

That's just the way it's wired. And when we are not intentionally focusing our attention on any one part of the present, it's going to take that decision from us and focus on what it wants to: things that generally cause you stress.

Now you may be thinking, yeah but isn't it helpful to plan for the future or understand where you went wrong in a situation so it doesn't happen again?

Absolutely!

But there comes a point when our musings and planning and attempts to understand shift from being helpful to being just another way we try to make ourselves feel better through attempts to control our minds and escape our realities.

That first list we make or ten minutes spent planning for a future probable event?

Super helpful.

The fourth time we do it?

Not so much.

Sooner or later we find ourselves right back in that sneaky pattern of avoidance and control that we talked about in Part I. And we know that doesn't work. Dan Harris, best selling author of *10% Happier* and host of Nightline and Good Morning America, explains this distinction well in *Minimalism: A documentary about important things*,

> *"I realized that there is a certain amount of worrying that is what I call 'constructive anguish' and then there's just useless rumination that's just making you miserable."*

Well said Dan, well said.

So what do we do? We train our minds to notice when we are stuck in a control loop and learn to shift our attention to what is happening in the present moment. After all, the only influence you have to change anything in your life is in this moment right now.

You can plan how you may respond in a future situation, but you can only act in the present.

Remember too that the purpose of this practice, the reason we are training our minds, lies in the knowledge that control strategies do not work in the long term to take us closer to the life we want to live and through practice we can begin to slow down, notice what unpleasant stuff is showing up for us, and create space to choose how we react.

I want you to have control over your life, even if you don't always have control over when stress shows up.

I want you to be able to choose, even in the midst of intense emotions, thoughts, or sensations, what you want to be about in this moment.

I want you to be able to engage in something meaningful to you that will help propel you forward into a future that is rich and fulfilling regardless of the chaos in your life.

This new practice does not happen overnight. Strengthening new habits for the mind takes repetition. Just as we do not go to the gym once and declare ourselves fit, we cannot expect to have complete mastery of our attention with minimal effort.

Instead of viewing this skill as a race to finish or an assignment to complete, know that it is not something you will ever finish as your mind has an agenda of its own. Rather learning to intentionally direct your attention is a continuous journey, a daily practice, to bring your mind back to noticing what matters in this moment over and over again in order to give you choice over your next move.

Sometimes that experience will be effortless, other times painful. But every time it will be focusing your attention for one more moment on something that is important to you and helping you perform better in the long run.

Let's try a little focusing exercise. Really, stop reading and try it right now.

> Look around wherever you are and identify five things you can see . . .
>
> Reach out and touch four different objects, really feeling the various textures of every object . . .
>
> Next, try noticing three different sounds you hear whether within the space you're in or maybe further in the distance . . .
>
> Take a deep breath and see if you can identify two smells; maybe your hair or shirt has a scent different from that in the room . . .
>
> And finally, taste something (something that is safe to taste)—just please don't lick anyone.

What was that like? Did you feel a thought creep in that said, "*this is ridiculous*"? Or "*I have better things to do with my time*"? Isn't it cool that even when we are aware of it, our minds keep trying to take us from the present moment in subtle ways?

That was a simple focusing exercise, a way to pull us out of our minds and into the moment. If you keep going, keep continuously redirecting your attention to your own experience around you you'll greatly widen your awareness so that you begin to recognize not only the impact being present has on your life, but also the costs of spending your life stuck in your head creating monsters out of shadows and losing out on people who matter to you, ideas that were never developed, and time that you can never get back.

I'd be a hypocrite if I didn't practice myself. I try to do formal mindfulness practice every day for at least ten minutes and practice informally throughout; In reality I tend to practice mindfulness about 4-5 days per week, and on days when I'm not as successful I notice it: I'm just a tiny bit more sucked into my thoughts and feelings, a little more on edge, irritated more easily by the small things, struggling to be a good listener, and distracted from my work.

So what can you do to begin your practice?

Remove distractions and immerse yourself in one task. These days our lives are consumed with juggling a dozen different balls at once. And this is so normal now that we don't see how problematic it is.

But every time we switch our attention between a task at work to the ding of our cellphone or between our kids and the television we lose focus and time—and those moments add up, creating a lot of time wasted and a dip in performance no matter the activity.

So create a context for full immersion: turn off all alerts on your phone and computer, remove social media apps or bookmarks so you can't get lost down an internet rabbit hole, shut off the television or radio when talking to others and put your full attention into hearing them, and for everyone's safety please put down your phone while driving, I promise you are not the exception to the rule.

The goal is simple: set yourself up for success. Below I've summarized some different strategies to practice honing your attention. I've made sure to include activities that don't require being seated in a quiet room and a variety of guided and self-directed practices. I'd encourage you to set an intention to try out different ones or include a combination of many in your everyday routine.

Download an app or peruse YouTube if you're looking for a more guided practice where you are given instructions to direct your attention in a specific way. My favorite app is Headspace—they have ten free, 10 minute sessions plus other fancier paid subscriptions and are very consistent with the philosophy we have been exploring in this book; I only use the free sessions and simply repeat over and over, but there are many mindfulness apps out there to try. Why not try them all!

Busy Mind Insiders who subscribe to my mailing list at www.busymindreboot.com get access to downloadable guided meditations for free.

Notice five things either you see, smell, taste, hear, or feel. As we demonstrated earlier, we automatically filter out so much in our environment that you can be in a place you've been dozens if not hundreds of times and notice nothing, or pause once and notice so many things you've never noticed before. Tip: try this while doing a chore or behavior you do regularly without much thought such as while taking a shower, brushing your teeth, or washing the dishes. You may be surprised by all of the sensory experiences you've been missing out on.

Go outside and take a breath and look around. Seriously. Take a breath and then pay attention. Maybe you'll see a colorful street sign, or hear the whirr of the A/C unit. Maybe you'll smell the rain or flowers or a car exhaust.

Maybe you'll feel the heat against your skin or the biting cold of the wind on your cheeks. It does not need to be something profound, it simply needs to be something present. Mindful walking is one of those strategies that hits the trifecta: fresh air, exercise, and present moment awareness.

Whether you are walking around your neighborhood, from your car into a store to run errands, or taking a hike in a park you can begin to notice and appreciate many different sensations you otherwise would have missed. It doesn't need to take any extra time. You do not have to walk at a leisurely pace or go out of your way to take a walk somewhere.

I am guessing that you are moving to and from somewhere a few times a day even if it's simply from the couch to the bathroom. Use that as an opportunity to notice. What does it feel like to shift your weight from one foot to the other as you walk? How do you hold your arms as you move?

If you are using some type of assisted device to move from one place to the other notice where you distribute your weight to feel most stable. Use the following mindful walking script as a guide if that helps. Always remember, mindfulness, being mindful, or simply aware of the present moment, is an approach to engaging with the world and yourself, and as such has no limitations on how it can be done.

For those who are unable to stand or walk without assistance, but rather move using a wheelchair or similar device, please alter the language used when the exercise refers to standing or feeling your feet on the ground to instead notice the different sensations of your body in the chair, or focusing on areas of sensation as you move forward. This is an eyes open exercise.

This shouldn't need to be said, but in case it does, please take appropriate cautions when walking in busy areas or near traffic. This is not a trust exercise.

Begin in a standing upright position, if comfortable, bringing your shoulders up to your ears and then gently rolling them back and down. Notice your breath expanding your chest and belly with each inhale and releasing with each exhale. Before moving, simply notice your intention to walk mindfully, bringing full attention to the sensations of both your body and the world around you.

First, notice your feet in your shoes and the points where they touch the inside of your shoes. . . . Begin to walk at a slow, leisurely pace, feeling with each step your heel touching the ground first and then the rest of your foot rolling down into the floor, followed by the sensation of your heel lifting from the ground, leaving the pad of your foot and toes the last part touching the ground. . . . Pay attention to the places on the bottoms of your feet that touch the ground as you walk, not trying to change or alter your pace or step in any way.

Practice simply noticing your walk for a minute or two.

Turn your attention to the sensations against your skin: Is there a breeze or heat pulsing against you? Do you feel warm sunshine or cool breeze or wet rain? Notice the different sensations and temperatures. Do you feel a difference between exposed skin and skin hidden beneath clothing?

Practice simply feeling different sensations for a minute or two.

Next, look around you, noticing the colors, textures, and shapes you see. . . . Allow your eyes to linger on anything that interests you and then continue on to the next, constantly observing all the details of your environment. . . . If your mind begins to wander or chatter about what it sees, simply notice that and return your attention to the sights around you.

Practice simply seeing what is around you for a minute or two.

Now, allow your ears to open wide, picking up the sounds of your feet taking each step. . . . Notice the sounds nearby and those far away. . . . Can you hear the different volumes and tones in the sounds around you? Notice both the separate distinct sounds and how they all sound together.

Practice simply listening to what is around you for a minute or two.

Finally, bring all of these experiences together: your feet in your shoes taking each step, the sensations along your skin as you walk, the different sights around you, and all the sounds you hear both near and far away. . . . Notice too any thoughts or feelings that arise as you practice, acknowledging these as part of the experience of observing and turning your attention back to your walk. . . . When safe to do so bring your body to a stop, noticing how your body feels at rest, scanning the body down to your feet in your shoes. . . . Feel the pace of your breath flowing in and out . . . and notice your intention to pause your mindful walk.

How did that go? Take a moment to reflect on the experience of walking mindfully.

Listen with effort. We all do it: have half a conversation with someone while thinking of our next task for the day. Instead, try really hearing the other person and putting yourself in their mind behind their eyes.

The next person you interact with, whether it's a loved one or the barista at Starbucks, really pay attention to what they are saying and pause to avoid answering with a remote response. As you're talking see if you can put yourself in their shoes so to speak. If you were looking behind their eyes what would you see? What sensations would you be feeling? Would you feel heard?

One of my favorite things in the whole world is eating delicious foods. It sounds so simple or mundane compared to the exotic or thrilling potential of life, but give me a good meal and I'm happy.

I try to take every moment to savor that experience. But that didn't always use to be the case. I'm not quite sure how I developed the habit as I didn't grow up in a large family fighting over the last dinner roll, I am grateful I have never worried where my next meal was coming from, and I have never been in a regimented environment like the military where I had to scarf down food in ten minutes or else I didn't get to eat, but I used to eat really fast.

Honestly, I'm legitimately surprised I never choked on my food given how quickly I'd inhale it. It was as if I enjoyed the food so much that I wanted it to disappear quickly and barely taste it. Doesn't make much sense, but that was the gist of things in my life.

Then in my graduate training, I facilitated a 90-minute workshop to help college students reduce added sugar consumption and as part of that experience I started training others in the practice of mindful eating.

Oh, the irony!

We did this training using raisins, which is a common mindful eating practice food for some reason. I'm guessing this practice began as raisins are pretty bland, have an incredible shelf life, and while some folks aren't huge fans of raisins, they rarely make it to the top of anyone's favorites or most hated foods lists. The idea was to take something pretty 'meh' and see if we could expand our awareness enough to notice subtleties in the sensory experience of the raisin.

As I refuse to be responsible for anyone finding a long-expired box of hard raisins ten years from now with only a few raisins missing, I would suggest using a food you really enjoy to practice this skill.

Maybe a small piece of chocolate, a pretzel, your favorite childhood dish, really it does not matter what you pick as long as you are willing to eat it. The idea is to connect to the process of eating while engaging all of your senses.

What does the food look like? Does it have a smell? Can you hear it as you chew or swallow or does it crackle or sizzle before eating it? Is there a particular texture you associate with it? And finally what does it taste like?

We want to approach food as if we're just now discovering it and want to slow down and take a closer look. You don't have to eat like a slowly munching panda bear or place your fork down between each bite and be that person who moans when they eat.

Rather while we may exaggerate the slowness when purposefully practicing an exercise, even when you are pressed for time there is an opportunity to notice what is happening as you consume food or beverage. Read through the following mindful eating script and give it a go the next time you sit down, stand at the sink, or hunch over your desk to eat.

1. Take the food and hold it (or the plate it is on) in your hand. Is it cool, neutral in temperature, or warm to the touch? Is it soft or firm?

2. Look at it closely. Is it uniform in color? Uneven? Flawed or unflawed? Is there a noticeable pattern or design on it?

3. Does it make any sound as you hold it or move it between your fingers?

4. Examine the food as if you've never encountered it before. Wonder about it—what is it? Where did it come from? How was it made or grown?

5. Now smell the food. Does it have a scent, or is it odorless?

6. Notice any urges to eat it. Do you have any sense of impatience, thoughts, feelings, or desires?

7. Be aware of your conscious decision to eat this food. Note any thoughts or feelings. Do you feel any sense of excitement?

8. Now put the food in your mouth and let it rest on your tongue. What does it taste like before you bite down? What is the texture like? How does it feel on your tongue? Is it rough or smooth? Does it taste sweet or salty?

9. Bite into the food. Chew it slowly. How does the flavor change? Does it make a sound as you bite into it? Is the texture the same?

10. Does this food evoke any feelings or memories? Practice being aware of the distinctions between the sensations in the moment and all the thoughts and feelings evoked by the act of eating.

11. After swallowing, pause to notice any changes in the sensations of hunger or satisfaction of your appetite.

12. Once you've finished eating the food, pause and reflect on the experience. Notice any thoughts of "wanting more" or any feelings of "having enough." What else can you be aware of before your transition to your next activity?

And breathe. Have you ever seen a toddler take a nap on their back? Ever noticed the rising and falling of their belly, like a giant balloon being inflated and deflated over and over again.

A curious thing happens as we get older. We lose that practice of breathing. Instead, our shoulders tighten in tension, often curling forward over our desks or rising up to our ears in duress. That hunched over position or stiff posture restricts our diaphragm from expanding, making our chest and shoulders rise and fall, and our breaths shallow and rushed.

This tension can increase our blood pressure, cause strain, and other physical symptoms like headaches over time.

Other times we take large exaggerated deep breaths thinking that will help us calm down. Believe it or not, research has found this can feed the cycle of stress by making you feel out of breath, faint, or lightheaded, which in turn makes you even more anxious or stressed.

Another excellent example of how our efforts to control make us more out of control.

Sometimes we even hold our breath when we are stressed! When you notice you are feeling stressed, stop for a moment to see if you are breathing.

Take a moment right now to pause and place one hand on your chest and one on your belly (or if unable to simply turn your attention to these areas) and notice which hand moves more as you breathe, resisting any temptation to modify or control your breathing. For most of us, if we're truly breathing as we usually do, that hand on our belly does not rise that high.

Now, this time breathe in. Pause. And release. No need to exaggerate your breath or slow it down in any way. Simply breathe. Watch your hands as you inhale and exhale. See if you can feel the air filling your diaphragm and pushing your belly out like a balloon as you breathe in. If you're still having difficulty, push your shoulders up to your ears and then slowly roll them back, allowing more space for your body to fill with air. What do you notice?

A simple strategy for grounding ourselves in the present moment is to breathe to a count of ten: one with the inhale, two with the exhale until you hit ten. This simple awareness of breath can be a quick strategy for creating some space between you and your mind.

I have a downloadable guided mindful breathing exercise in

the free resources section of my website www.busymin-dreboot.com available exclusively to Busy Mind Insider subscribers if listening to someone (me!) guide you through an exercise is helpful.

It may seem like a small thing, a breath, but sometimes all we need is one moment to be here, now.

Putting practice into action—pick one strategy to practice every day for the next week for a total of ten minutes per day. Try to tie this practice to something you regularly do. Here are some examples: "when I brush my teeth, then I will take the full two minutes of brushing to be present," "if I go for a walk, then I will practice mindful walking," "when I get in bed to go to sleep, then I will play the guided body scan meditation from Busy Mind Reboot website," "if I get up to go to the restroom, then I will notice my breath for a count of ten when I sit back down."

Now, you try it!

When/If I _____ ,

Then I will _____.

Tip: set a reminder on your phone, write it into your calendar or planner, put a sticky note on your computer, fridge or mirror. Find a way to remind yourself to do it otherwise you are bound to get swept away by the day and forget.

3

THE SAME 24 HOURS

So you've taken the time to identify how stress presents itself in your life and have begun a regular mindfulness practice?

Great!

But a little voice in the back of your head keeps says, "yes, but" and that "yes, but" can end in many ways: yes, but I don't have time; yes, but I have too many responsibilities; yes, but it's too hard; yes, but there are things in my life preventing me from living the life I want to have.

I would never say that these reasons are not valid, that they are simply things our minds have constructed, and yet often these "yet, buts" are not the insurmountable obstacles we believe them to be.

Let's take a look at some of these obstacles to self-care, slowing down, and focusing on what matters.

1. I don't have time.

When people say they don't have time, what they really mean is that this activity or person is not a priority in their lives.

Now, that sounds harsh, and I don't mean to be, but in reality we all have 24 hours in a day and we each choose different ways to spend that time. It's like having a big pie divided into 24 slices: one person may have a pie that has 15 slices of work, 5 slices of sleep, 1 slice of shower and breakfast, 1 slice of dinner, and 2 slices of spending time with the kids (or getting lost down the proverbial internet rabbit hole).

If that person wanted to add in seeing friends to their busy schedule they couldn't just add another slice, there isn't room. They would have to remove one slice in order to add another.

When you say you don't have time for something you are effectively saying you have already used up the hours in your day for something else. Whether that something else is meaningful or valuable to you is another question entirely.

Now, we are pretty terrible at recall: remembering things that happened in the past, even as recent as 24 hours ago, so in order to get an accurate idea of your slices of pie you'll need to intentionally track those hours. I'd recommend keeping a piece of paper in your pocket, creating an excel document, or writing notes in your phone to track how you spend your time every day for a week. It may sound extreme, however tracking what you are doing every 15 minutes—obviously not when you are asleep—can be an accurate way to see what types of slices are in your 24-hour pie. Compare that to the list you made of who and what matter most to you as part of your action steps for Part I.

Are you spending your time doing things that take you closer to what matters most to you?

Keep in mind that this is not a list of what you like or how you want to spend your time. For instance, working two jobs may be a step towards your family, who matter a great deal to you, even if you don't get to spend a lot of time with them because through working you are able to provide for them and ensure they are safe.

Are your slices of pie a representation of what matters most to you?

We can very easily fall into a trap where we convince ourselves that how we spend our time takes us closer to what matters when really all it is doing is helping us escape unpleasant thoughts, feelings, memories, and physical sensations. Maybe you're working two jobs because you fear your children will be made fun of if they don't have every gadget other kids have or can't play on a travel sports team when in reality spending time with your children is more important than extracurriculars.

Maybe you feel distanced from your partner or that your family would be better off without you so you remove yourself from the situation by working a lot. **The same action can serve different functions depending on the situation.**

So take a hard look: is how you are spending your time working for you?

Is it taking you closer to what matters most to you?

And if not, which slices can you swap out and how?

That's not an answer I can provide. You are the only person who can determine if your actions are working for you.

2. I have too many responsibilities

Sometimes, not always, but **sometimes we use responsibility as a way to avoid our own lives.** And it's hard to stop because it's very reinforcing: we get praise or feel good for doing something for someone else or helping out someone who could use an extra hand. But it can come at a cost if we spend all of our time focused on others and not enough time focused on ourselves.

It is why those in helping professions have such high rates of burnout: **you can't give to others if you don't have anything left in the tank to give.**

Parents also struggle with this concept. So instead of trying to convince you maybe I can ask a simple question: Are you setting the type of example you want for your children? Are you teaching them to take care of themselves and enjoy their lives and the people in them?

If it is the case that you have a lot of responsibilities, take some time to think about whether these responsibilities in the long-term are taking you closer to the life you want to live. Maybe you are taking care of your aging parents in addition to working, but this increase in stress is worth it because your parents are important to you. **Sometimes understanding our actions in the context of chasing our values can make the stress seem more manageable or more purposeful.**

Are there opportunities to share the responsibilities with others?

One difficulty with modifying responsibilities is we have this notion that we either a) will disappoint someone or b) will have to set firm boundaries with someone, usually family members. And unfortunately, I can't guarantee both won't happen. These two barriers can feel so unpleasant or aversive that we tend to shoulder the responsibilities even if it's not what we want to be doing (and it causes us a lot of stress).

Are you willing to make changes in your responsibilities so that you can spend more time on what you care about?

3. It's too hard

Of course it's hard, it matters to you. Inside our pain is where we find what truly matters to us.

And maybe I misheard you and you don't mean hard as in emotionally, but rather the task or action seems over-whelming or with a low probability of success: it's possible you're right.

We often try to tackle way too much at a time, setting our sights to be perfect or some robotic machine that never stops or takes breaks. That's setting yourself up for failure plain and simple. Not because you're a failure, but because any new change in our behavior is going to be really difficult at first as there was a reason you were doing something else in its place; it felt good to avoid or escape or say yes all the time. Even if only for a moment followed by regret. So changing even in minuscule ways is going to be a struggle.

For example, I found myself in a writing rut lately, procrasti-nating on even the simplest tasks because this book is important to me and I had thoughts and worries about my ability to deliver a book that met my goals of providing prac-tical advice to help those who need it. These worries created a sense of apprehension and anxiety in me to the point that even opening up this document to write seemed overwhelming and I found myself binge-watching Netflix or cleaning my home, again.

How did I overcome this obstacle? I set a goal to write 100 words every day. If I wrote more than that? Fantastic! But my goal was to write 100. To give you a reference for how small that goal was, this brief paragraph is 133 words. I may have felt silly at times for writing a sentence or two and hitting my goal, but the point was I took a difficult and overwhelming task, a hard task, and broke it down into something so small I knew I couldn't fail. I know some authors who set goals of 50 words per day, and sometimes they have days of 50 words and sometimes 3,000 words, but the point is they found a way to create a consistent change that before seemed too hard.

So what's hard about the changes you want to make that will improve your quality of life?

Seriously, what's hard about them?

What would doing ten percent of that look like?

Does that seem more manageable?

If yes, congratulations you found your new task.

If no, what does ten percent of ten percent of the changes you want to make look like?

Remember folks, **progress is made one step at a time**, always. Even tiny steps move us forward and add up in the long run.

4. If I can't do it X, then there's no reason to do it.

I hear this most often when it comes to exercise. I'm not quite sure why, but we tend to have very strict rules about what exercise is. For example, some people think it only counts as exercise if you sweat, others feel silly if they go to the gym for less than an hour. And as a result, none of them exercise. Why? Because they can't devote an entire slice of pie to exercise every day (or even once per week) and with such a narrow view of what exercise is they don't have any alternatives.

I'm sure you can think of different examples where this "If I can't do it this way then there's no point in doing it" rigidity pops up in your life.

If not, take a moment to think of the experiences or actions you would like to do more of that would take you in the direction of a meaningful life for you and contemplate why you aren't doing them. It's likely you'll stumble across one or two rules.

We call this black and white thinking or being rigid. It's great to have a plan or an ideal. It's bad if that's the only way you can do that activity.

To expand on the exercise example above: 10 minutes of exercise per day is better than no minutes per day. Full stop. Period. 100 extra steps are better than the same amount of steps you did the day before. Sure, it doesn't come with a glow of achievement or the feeling of making it to the top of the mountain, but **we aren't doing the behavior to feel a certain way.** At least I'm not. I'm doing it because it's important to me. Think on that.

5. Something in my life (external barrier) is preventing me from doing it

We spend a lot of time in this book examining our own patterns of behavior because frankly, that's what we have the most influence over. Sometimes, however, it's a little more complicated than that. There are a couple of external barriers that we often cite that get in the way of chasing our dreams and reducing our stress.

Lack of time: see #1

Responsibilities: see #2

Other people. Other people can be great; they can also suck. Suck our time. Suck our energy. Suck our souls. If you have such a person in your life take an honest look at your relationship and ask yourself some difficult questions: what patterns of interacting do I have with this person? How am I contributing to difficult situations and what could I do differently that's within the scope of my values? What boundaries do I need to set with this person? And finally, the most difficult of all, should this person be in my life?

Situational barriers. How can we problem solve this situation to get what we want? Sometimes it involves a combination of the three previous solutions, and sometimes we need to get creative. What has always helped me is to sit down and identify what the actual problem is. Is it a conflict with a co-worker, a difficult child care routine, conflicting messages from upper management, a long commute? Write down what the actual issue is.

Sometimes seeing it on paper can help you see it clearly. I have found that what we often believe to be the problem is really more stories in our mind and when we get the practical information down on paper we are able to discern what the actual components that make up the issue are. Once we have a good idea of the issue and the moving parts we can begin to brainstorm.

Let me be clear here: "I don't know" is not a solution. Write it down at the top of your list if you must, but write some more words below it. **Take 3 minutes to write down every single possible solution to the problem** even if it seems unlikely to work or to cause additional problems. Get creative. Can you pay someone to make it easier or free up more of your time? Can you barter with someone to exchange certain tasks? Can you team up with someone to spread the impact or get backup support?

I like the 3-minute rule because minute one is for every idea you have already thought of, minute two is for common or typical ideas, and minute three is where the magic happens. Where we have those "oh my gosh I can't believe I never thought to do that, that would definitely work" moments. So take some paper and a pen and a stopwatch on your phone and start brainstorming. There is always a solution out there because basically at the end of the day we always find ourselves in the same situations.

With any inquiry about how we manage our time, there are either two things happening.

1. **What you say you want to be spending your time doing is not a priority to you.** It happens. Sometimes we get so caught up in "*shoulds*" or "*musts*" that we frankly have no idea what's important to us. Again, that's why taking time to figure out who and what matter to you is so important. We

can't get to a destination if we don't know where we want to go.

2. You are avoiding unpleasant experiences (thoughts, feelings, memories, physical sensations, specific places or people, or activities) through focusing on others, on perceived responsibilities, or on meaningless, or less important tasks. We are great at procrastinating, making up excuses, being really excellent at something that in the grand scheme of things doesn't matter while we let what truly matters to us wilt and die.

And it makes sense in a twisted sort of way: having people, activities, qualities that matter to us is scary because it also means we can lose them or be hurt by them. So we fill our time, use our slices of the pie, for stuff that's less threatening because to move towards what matters we also move towards a place of vulnerability, a place of potentially getting hurt.

This concept can be understood using an experience I'd wager you have had: procrastination.

For example, this book is important to me. I've outlined the reasons why previously. So every time I go to write, my mind tells me it's going to be terrible, that the outcomes I hope for won't happen, and I'll have wasted a huge amount of time for nothing. Sometimes my body fills me with weight, making me feel heavy and tired: "too tired" to get any work done.

And almost as if I called the image into my mind, I start thinking about some random television show on Netflix or imagine cozying up in my pajamas on the couch. Maybe my mind starts whispering to me, *"this book is going to be terrible"* and suddenly I feel the need to clean the entire house including cleaning out the fridge, sorting the pantry, and making lists, endless lists.

The problem is every time we give in to that immediate pleasure of distraction or avoidance we reinforce all the anxiety, self-defeating thoughts, and general despondency. So the next time I go to write, there it is! And it's larger than it was before.

We fear the fear so we do any and everything we can to avoid it, even if it means not moving toward the life we want to live.

Don't worry though. Everyone does it. But with a little knowledge, we can catch these moments happening and break the cycle.

———

So we've sorted out some of our time wasters, but you still feel a bit disorganized. That's okay, we could all benefit from some simple time management strategies. I've written down the most common and most valuable ones for you to implement in your life to get more done and carve out a slice for what really matters.

1. **Focus on one task at a time.** Everyone likes to think they are multitaskers, but I can almost guarantee you are not the exception to the rule. The concept of multitasking has been studied and debunked.

When people say they are multitasking what they are really doing is switching their attention back and forth between two tasks. The problem with this is that not enough directed attention is focused on any given task and as a result, both tasks end up taking longer than if you had done them sequentially, one after the other, rather than trying to complete both at the same time.

2. Put down the phone, close the laptop, turn off the television, unplug the music. Distractions, similar to multitasking, divert our attention away from our main objective. If you find yourself struggling to pay attention to one thing for a long period of time break it up into ten or fifteen-minute chunks. But stay on task for those ten or fifteen minutes.

3. As mentioned before, procrastination sucks, and it leads to a lot of "I'll do it later" moments in life. That's why I am a huge proponent of **getting the difficult stuff done first thing when you wake up.** This includes stress management strategies that are a struggle to put into practice such as a daily meditation routine.

For me, I know if I want to meditate regularly, then I have to do it in the morning. I'll tell myself I can do it during a brief break in the day, but there's always something that comes up: an email I have to reply to, a phone call I have to take, scrolling through Instagram.

Then, I'll tell myself I'll do it before bed, but generally fall asleep in the middle of it which kind of defeats the purpose. The bottom line is, if you can, knock out stressful tasks first thing so you aren't spending all day worrying about it or making "*I'll do it later*" remarks with a dash of guilt sprinkled in.

Get it over with. You'll thank yourself, feel accomplished, and get a little boost of energy to carry you through whatever else the day has in store for you.

4. I remember when I first figured out my cell phone had email on it. It was a blackberry my stepmom had given me when she got a new phone and it took me four months before someone pointed out the feature to me. I was amazed. I was in university at the time and didn't get that many emails. So much has changed since then. I have four email addresses—FOUR—with three that I check daily. All connected to my phone. I've considered tracking how many times per day I check my email, but I never have out of embarrassment; it must be well over 50 times per day. And while it is important for me to check my email daily, even a few times per day, I've come to realize I spend a lot of my waking hours checking emails that didn't need to be dealt with.

If you're like me, and you have something in your life you do over and over again that not only doesn't make your life easier but causes additional stress and disruptions: it's time to stop now. For me, the big change was when I read Tim Ferris's book, *The Four Hour Work Week*. He suggested having one or two periods per day that you check and answer emails and limit checking email to those time blocks only.

And I have to say it worked. All those 1-2 minute moments of getting sucked into my phone were now mine again. And I found better uses for them: listened to a song I liked, wrote a few sentences in a book I was working on, created a grocery list, sent a message to someone I love; All activities I could do using my phone that made my life better. That reduced rather than added stress. Those moments add up. So **what habits are you holding on to that don't serve a purpose and only add stress?**

5. Schedule breaks for your mind, body, and soul. Sitting at a desk all day or completing the same mind-numbingly dull task over and over again can feel defeating to even the chirpiest of us all. Before you start telling me how your boss will kill you if you are not chained to your desk, bear with me. I'm not saying do any less work unless that is a choice you are making towards your values. What I am saying is this: our minds are not meant to work for hours on end and all the evidence points to this being a terrible strategy for completing tasks.

You should be focusing on one task for no more than 45 minutes then taking a mini break before getting back to the grind.

Breaks can look different depending on what you need in that moment to help you settle down and step back from the stress storm brewing in your mind or body.

Maybe you get up to say hello to a co-worker, or take a lap around the office as you pretend to print a document or ask a question. Maybe you do a little stretch at your desk raising your hands above your head or pause and watch your breath for a few inhales and exhales, finishing off the moment looking around the office and observing. Maybe you put your headphones in and listen to that one song that makes you smile and tap your foot.

It doesn't have to be life-altering or even productive. The goal is to recharge a little so that you can be a better you when you turn back to your work and so that you aren't drained at the end of the day.

6. Create a list of three things you must get done and only focus on that, the rest is a bonus. We hurt ourselves when we make pages of to-do lists. It seems so overwhelming even small movement feels like a failure. So take the pressure off.

Identify the top three things you MUST get done today leaving all the "*it would be nice to have this done*" off. Complete those three items. Do more afterward if you want, but I really don't care either way. Just do those three things.

Now, let's see what all of this looks like in practice.

Take Richard for example. Richard was in his mid-40s, married, two children at home, and had a successful career with a terrible commute. When I first met Richard he told me that he would love to exercise more as his family has a history of heart disease and his father died from a heart attack, but with his busy life and long commute it just wasn't possible. He described waking up at 5:30 am, getting dressed and helping get the kids ready for school. He'd be out the door at 6:40 am, drop the kids off, then have an hour long commute into work. Richard would then work at a desk all day and leave at around 5:30 pm and hit rush hour traffic which led to an hour and fifteen-minute commute home. Once home he'd have dinner with his family, help his kids with any remaining homework and tuck them into bed, then flop on the couch with his wife for a little television and downtime before passing out to start all over again.

He explained to me that his weekends weren't any better as he was usually spending some time catching up on emails, chauffeuring the kids to different activities, running errands, paying bills, and generally doing everything he could just to keep up. So what could he possibly do to steal back some of that time for his health? Well, Richard knew he couldn't leave work early to miss any traffic, but once he started poking around with different times leaving work he realized that if he left work at 6:00 pm (half an hour later than usual) his commute was cut down to 45 minutes allowing him to arrive at home at the same time and have 30 minutes to exercise at work.

While there wasn't a gym near his office there were sidewalks, and beginning twice a week to test it out, Richard changed into exercise clothes after work and went on a 30-minute walk/jog. After a while, that habit turned into running for 30 minutes after work five days per week. While there were days when he skipped exercising or still hit major traffic on his drive home, overall he was able to get that minimum 150 minutes of aerobic exercise to stay healthy and prevent future health concerns.

Richard's story is a great example of the typical busy lifestyle for families these days. Add in an unrelenting boss, or a single parent with lack of help at home and very easily a difficult scenario can feel like an impossible one. And yet there is always an opportunity to make small changes to our routine to move towards the life we want to have.

Megan had one of those impossible scenarios: feeling as though there was no time to squeeze out for herself all the while creeping closer and closer to a breakdown from work stress, home stress, and everything in between. We worked together to write a list of various self-care or relaxation activities she could do in one-minute, five-minute, and ten-minute periods, and intentionally schedule them into her day.

She started with waking up ten minutes early and sitting down to drink a cup of tea by herself before starting her hectic day. Those few minutes with her warm cup of tea in the quiet house helped her feel centered and ready to tackle the frustrating routine of getting her kids ready for school and out the door on time. On her drive to work, she'd listen to music she enjoyed, singing along even if she didn't feel like it. She found that after she started she would laugh at how silly she felt and a smile would break out on her face. Then, when she parked her car before going into her job where'd she'd have to navigate disgruntled employees all day, she would focus on her breath for a count of ten: breathe in (1), breathe out (2) all the way to 10.

Megan explained that her job was extremely stressful because people would call her or come to her office often really upset and even though she didn't create the problem she was the point person they talked to and therefore the person they took out their frustration on. She would describe how she knew they weren't really mad at her and honestly they usually had a legitimate reason to be upset, but when hour after hour you get yelled at it's hard to keep that perspective. So we devised a plan to help: she wrote out different words or phrases to represent why employees might be upset (no time, our companies fault), and stuck them to her computer along with qualities she wanted to be about in that moment (kind, helpful, good listener, patient); a small reminder to get a new perspective.

It may not seem like it, but these small changes make a big difference over time and help to take that edge off of stress and take back some time for yourself. Tiny changes that feel almost too small to even do can often be an excellent place to start as they are generally pretty easy for us to work into our schedules and we feel more ridiculous not being able to make them work than doing them.

How will you take back your 24 hours?

Putting practice into action—

1. What is one tiny change you can make in your schedule to move towards something that is important to you?

2. How will you remind yourself to do this behavior?

3. How will you track this behavior?

4

DON'T OPERATE HEAVY MACHINERY

SLEEP IS a necessity for human survival.

We require it to consolidate memory, taking what we learned throughout the day and storing it in our brain for later retrieval. We benefit from better concentration and focus which ultimately leads to improved productivity, freeing up more time for other activities and attending to all the information we need to stay on topic and succeed, such as when in a meeting or talking to a friend. We need sleep for recovery, staying strong, and healing. And finally, we demand sleep to be a pleasant, friendly person others want to be around.

All that being said, in our current culture and society we tend to undervalue sleep or act as though is it something that can be shortchanged now and caught up on in the future—you know, once this one stressor is gone. Of course, there's always something else that comes up and gets in the way.

I want to caution that a few nights of poor or limited sleep will not leave you incapable of functioning. And there are many other sources of daytime grogginess or lack of focus: exercise, dehydration, decreased time spent outside in the sun, poor nutrition, a cold or other illness, and of course, stress.

Not to mention the impact stress has on your sleep to begin with. Suffice it to say, a book on stress wouldn't be complete without some serious devotion to the topic of sleep. In Part 4 I will walk you through simple strategies for improving your sleep and setting yourself up for successfully tackling the day, but first, we need to tackle some myths about sleep.

There are many myths out there about sleep that have a serious impact on how you approach sleep and more importantly, how you evaluate your own sleep habits and patterns.

1. Everyone should get eight hours of sleep per night. While there is an average amount of sleep people prefer throughout life (10 or more in childhood and adolescence, 8 hours in young adults and middle age, and 6 hours as you enter into older age) these are just that, averages. It would be hard to argue that your functional level of sleep is two hours per night or ten hours is necessary, but it could be the case that for you five or six hours of sleep keeps you feeling refreshed. Focusing on a specific number without evaluating your own patterns and preferences is a surefire way to make inaccurate adjustments to your sleep that leave you worse off in the end.

One important caveat to this is that any number you come up with should be based on sleep quality outside of any stimulants. **Caffeine is not a substitute for hours of sleep** and to make the claim that four hours of sleep is the perfect amount for you as you throw back your second, triple espresso latte of the morning is misguided.

2. If I feel groggy in the morning then I must not have gotten enough sleep. We tend to evaluate our sleep effectiveness and function based on how we feel first thing in the morning. The issue with this approach is that many if not most people feel groggy for the first 30 minutes of waking. For some, it may be lack of quality or quantity of sleep, but for many, it's simply part of how they greet the world.

It is far better to track how you feel a few hours after waking than when your eyes first open.

We all have natural dips in energy and increases in fatigue throughout the day. That is natural. But those who struggle to sleep may find themselves labeling these natural, recurring dips as proof of sleep difficulties which in turn lead to more frustration and stress followed by actual sleep problems. This tendency to misattribute stress or other factors in life as due to sleep deficit when really other causes are in play lead us to ignore the real culprits and as a result, we are unable to address these issues or make any meaningful changes in our lives.

3. Quantity is more important than quality of sleep.

> *How'd you sleep last night?*
> *Not great, I only got four hours of sleep.*
> *That's terrible! I can't function on less than eight.*

Does this sound like a familiar conversation? On a semi-regular basis we discuss sleep and it almost always comes down to two numbers: our ideal number and our reality.

Take a moment and think of what your two numbers are: ideal number and reality.

Now, I'm not doubting that you're dragging a bit after consistently sleeping only four hours per night, but if we tried we could likely find dozens of examples of functioning, even excelling, on the latter number. I know I have.

I still remember taking a red-eye from San Diego to Detroit, nodding in and out every thirty minutes for maybe a total of three hours of interrupted sleep only to take a shuttle to a hotel so I could get another hour of sleep before it was time to get up, shower, dress, and drive an hour south to defend my doctoral dissertation: a two-hour ordeal that was unequivocally the most important moment of my five years of hard work.

I nailed it!

The fact is that quality of sleep is more important than quantity. Don't get me wrong, over time poor quantity will get you, but if you can create a peaceful and consistent environment even those four hours will feel like eight. That's why as we go through different strategies for improving your sleep, and I encourage you to track your progress, I want you to restrain yourself from obsessively examining how many minutes of shut-eye you got and notice the quality, how you feel, once you start your day.

Who knows, it may surprise you.

———

Now that we've tackled sleep myths it's time to turn our attention to what you can do when faced with actual sleep struggles. Be warned this is not the place to cover all information and strategies about sleep. For those with chronic sleep disturbances I recommend reading my master guide to sleep: *Fall Asleep, Stay Asleep* (and consulting your doctor), but I do want to give you some starting tools to transform your sleep habits.

Even if you have struggled with sleep for years I urge, no *beg*, you to trial the strategies I will cover in the following pages.

I cannot tell you the number of clients who have reported years of challenges with sleep, who have told me to my face following treatment, "*I really didn't think this would work*," who gave me skeptical looks or exasperated sighs when I instructed them to track their sleep and make these small changes to their habits, and who ended up drastically improving both the quantity and quality of their sleep in a few short weeks.

Not everyone will fall into this category, and if you don't, know that there are effective ways for modifying sleep patterns in more severe cases, but you won't know which category you fall into until you give it a shot.

I recommend that you **track your sleep for one week to get a baseline of your habits**, including the following behaviors and how they influence your sleep, before attempting modifications. If you notice multiple areas of improvement or experimentation—I'm guessing you will—try making one change per week. That way you can see what helps and what doesn't. And because it's an experiment you can always go back to your old habits, just now you are doing it armed with the knowledge that you may suffer a decrease in sleep quality as a result.

You're an adult. You get to make that choice. My goal is to give you the information you need in order to make decisions that work for you and your goals.

Without further ado, strategies for improving sleep quality and quantity:

1. Cut the caffeine.

You know that third cup of coffee you have in the afternoon? The one that helps you pretend to be awake as you struggle to get over the post-lunch slump? Well, unfortunately, it can be contributing to your active mind at the end of the day.

Caffeine in any form: coffee, tea, soda, chocolate, acts as a stimulant and the effects can last for hours. I don't care how long you've been drinking coffee and how it *"doesn't affect me anymore."*

Humor me.

If you can't give up all caffeine, limit it to the mornings (if you have a traditional wake/sleep schedule), or try starting with one less cup of joe! The most important point is to **not have caffeine within six hours of attempting to fall asleep.** It can stay in your system for a while after consumption.

I worked with a guy named James once who had sleep difficulties for years and as an end of day ritual would drink one cup of tea. I think he only went along with stopping that cup of tea in order to not disappoint me. Turns out after substituting caffeinated tea with herbal tea in the evening and some other minor adjustments he was falling asleep within thirty minutes of going to bed and would wake up only once in the middle of the night on most evenings.

Don't estimate the power of stimulants.

2. Stop the smoke.

Similar to caffeine, nicotine can act as a stimulant keeping you wide awake and hyper in the evenings. Limiting smoking in general is a great idea for your health, but giving up that before bedtime smoke may help you fall asleep faster.

Not only do stimulants interfere with sleep, but they also can increase feelings of stress or anxiety. But wait, you say, I smoke in order to unwind.

I'm not doubting it helps in the moment. Generally, smokers find that even the act of reaching for a cigarette, lighting up, bringing it to their lips, or going outside to smoke causes an immediate relief.

The issue is it's not the actual smoke that's relaxing you, it's the habit or process of smoking. Think of how that cigarette is functioning in your life: does it give you a mini break from your work? An escape from your family? A bit of fresh air? A substitute for another craving (food, alcohol, other substances)?

Remember those questions we asked ourselves in Part I? If we take a hard look at how smoking is functioning or working in your life you begin to notice how smoking is really just another by-product, a short-term tool for coping with some long-term struggles.

And that's not even taking into account the nicotine dependence, which is no joke. Let's be clear, I am by no means suggesting quitting is easy. It's quite the opposite. But if you come to the conclusion that while it gives a short-term relief it comes with a high cost in the long-term consider alternative ways to meet that function and consult with your doctor on ways to ride out those nicotine cravings.

If you're smoking for general stress: test out other ways to unwind like listening to calming music, stretching, taking a bath, or reading a book.

If you're smoking for a mini break from the office: when you generally would take a smoke break, take a break! Get up and walk around, say hello to coworkers, look at cute puppies on Instagram, meditate. Giving up smoking doesn't mean giving up downtime.

If you're smoking to get some fresh air: take a walk. Sit outside. Just don't smoke while doing it.

If you're smoking to escape your family: consider what patterns you and family members have gotten into. Do you argue about the same topics over and over again? Do you sit in passive-aggressive niceness? Do you feel neglected or ignored? Are you neglecting or ignoring the other person? Again, take some time to identify what is happening.

This is not an opportunity to point out the other person's flaws or put the blame on someone else. Consider it a thought experiment: what changes can I make to share what is bothering me and show this person what they mean to me?

This isn't easy and won't change overnight, but every moment, every interaction, is an opportunity to set you on a different path and reconnect with those you love.

3. Manage medication.

Some asthma and weight loss medications also have stimulant effects. Talk to your doctor to find out whether any of your medications can interfere with sleep and see if your doctor approves taking the medication at a different time of day. *Never change how much or when you take any medication without first talking with your doctor as some medications need to be taken on a specific schedule or time of day.* I'm serious. Don't do it.

4. Avoid alcohol.

Need a nightcap to fall asleep? Many people use alcohol to fall asleep because it makes them drowsy. The problem with this approach is that while alcohol may help you fall asleep it actually leads to more restless sleep and greater chances of waking up throughout the night. This can happen with one drink in the evenings. Try avoiding alcohol for at least a week and monitor what happens particularly how many times you wake throughout the night.

If drinking in the evenings is part of a wind-down ritual for you try substituting the alcohol with an herbal tea or non-alcoholic beverage. You'll never find a better opportunity to try those fancy mocktail recipes! (Yes, I know, it's not the same. Doesn't mean it's not still enjoyable.)

5. Slow down the stress.

I imagine you wouldn't be reading this book if you weren't struggling with stress. While we can't always make our lives easier, we can take time to relax at the end of the day. Having a ritual for unwinding before bed can signal the brain that it's time for sleep. It doesn't need to be elaborate. Consider setting aside thirty minutes before bed for brushing your teeth, stretching, taking a hot bath, putting on lotion, meditating, reading, listening to relaxing music, or talking to your partner. Any and all of the above can make an impact.

6. No napping.

I remember working with a woman once who had been struggling with falling asleep in the evenings, often taking her two hours to fall asleep. As we went through her day and her evening routine it came out that she would nap for about thirty minutes on the train on her long commute home. She never considered that such a small nap could mess up her sleep so much.

The truth is that we all have a dip in energy at one point during the day (if you have a traditional sleep/wake schedule it's about 2:00 pm - 4:00 pm) where our sleep drive becomes stronger than our wake drive. The issue is if we give into that drive we essentially feed our sleep drive a little and when we are ready to go to sleep it's not as strong so it takes longer to wind down and fall asleep.

So don't nap. If you always fall asleep during a certain time of day, maybe on the couch or in your favorite chair, make sure you are not home during that time of day.

That's what I do. If I am home at 4:00 pm I will likely fall asleep or sit around and do nothing for an hour, so on days when I am not working at that time I run errands, work at a coffee shop or call my mom on the phone.

7. Stand up (and move).

Have you ever had that feeling where your mind is tired, but your body can't quite get comfortable? Sometimes our bodies need to feel tired to rest and sitting at a desk all day at work and then relaxing in front of the TV at home doesn't allow a lot of opportunity for your body to be active.

Taking a walk or going to the gym can increase your fatigue at the end of the day and make falling asleep a little easier. If you tend to feel energized after exercising, try to exercise at least a few hours before bed so you have time to unwind.

Exercise doesn't have to be strenuous. A leisurely walk outside in the sunshine could not only serve the purpose of keeping your body moving but also help reduce your stress. Being out in nature can help reduce stress and soaking in the sun during the day can help with maintaining an appropriate sleep/wake cycle so when it gets dark your brain knows it's time to sleep.

8. Select a standard wake-up time.

Use it every day regardless of the sleep you obtain on any particular night. This forces the body into a routine which increases the odds of consistent sleep.

9. Shut off the screens.

The blue light your television, computer, tablet, and phone emit can trick your brain into thinking it is daytime and delays the release of melatonin—the hormone that regulates sleep and wakefulness.

Some computers and phones have night modes that are either on the device or can be downloaded to change the blue tone to a warm color palette, and some reading tablets are not backlit.

For example, the Kindle I use does not have a backlight or search engine abilities. It is solely a device to read on and the image on the screen mimics real paper. Shut off the screens at least thirty minutes before bed. Take it a step further and dim or turn off other lights in your home as well. We want to start the process of slowing down and readying for sleep as early and easily as possible.

10. Bed is for sleep.

Television screens, traffic noise, extreme temperatures, and light can all adversely impact your sleep. Not to mention varying wake up times and naps. It's important to create a peaceful sleep environment. Make your bedroom as cozy, quiet, and dark as possible to help induce that drowsy comfortable feeling. And limit your bed to sleep and sex.

All too often our bed is where we read, watch television, even eat. With all this extra activity happening in bed our brains can begin to associate bed with excitement for a new television show or hunger for a good snack. Neither of which promote sleep or drowsiness. Take your television out of your bedroom and if you read before bed move that ritual to a chair or the couch. This way your brain will begin to associate bed with sleep, and it will be easier to fall asleep when you get into bed.

Above all, be patient. Your sleep problem developed over time so it will take some time to return to a more normal sleep pattern.

A note about doctors and medical conditions.

Sometimes medications or undiagnosed or poorly controlled chronic medical conditions can interfere with your sleep. For example, women who are going through menopause may report trouble falling or staying asleep. The same with people who have thyroid issues and therefore hormonal imbalances.

Similarly, I cannot tell you how many clients I have worked with who have sleep apnea but do not use their CPAP machine yet complain of sleep issues. I understand that a CPAP machine is frustrating and uncomfortable to use, but no amount of behavioral changes will counteract the fact that there is a medical condition causing your sleep difficulties.

The strategies I reviewed are great, but they are no substitute for managing medications, controlling medical conditions, and following recommended practices.

If you are suffering from chronic sleep difficulties and despite making changes to your routine and lifestyle continue to struggle please consult your doctor and describe your symptoms. Your doctor may recommend sleeping pills as a short-term solution as some sleep medications can become addictive and are not intended for long-term use, but it is also likely that they will assess whether your description of difficulties suggest another cause that can be otherwise controlled or managed.

And by a doctor, I mean a licensed medical professional. Not WebMD. In fact, it is my humble opinion that your life will be improved if you never use WebMD or other encyclopedias of medical problems. There was a joke I heard once about how when you consult WebMD you always end up having cancer. Our goal is to reduce stress, not create more stress with unsubstantiated claims and low probability of truth.

Putting practice into action—Spend the next couple weeks experimenting with the different tips we covered in Part 3. Reduce caffeine, cut out alcohol, eliminate blue screens before bed, set consistent sleep/wake patterns, and above all collect data on the results. Don't allow your mind to lull you into false beliefs about the outcome of these changes, focus on the actual hard facts. There are many sleep tracking logs available for free online (I created one available to Busy Mind Insiders) and I would recommend that you use some type of log, whether mine, one you find online, or one you create on your own to track your sleep progress.

5

WHAT'S THE POINT OF IT ALL?

So we've reached the final chapter: Part 5. I have done my best to provide you with tools you need to be successful in mastering your stress, whatever form it may take. By now hopefully you have given that mindfulness thing a shot, stolen back pieces of the time pie for what matters to you, and woken a little more rested and able to tackle the chaos.

This chapter veers away from offering practical strategies and skills. Because while the best information is necessary to move forward, knowledge alone does not make progress.

People make progress.

And fortunately and unfortunately people are not rational. They are driven by far more than facts and data and pros and cons lists.

We are driven by our hearts and our hopes and beliefs.

There was a reason you picked up this book. Maybe you're on a self-improvement binge. Maybe you are hoping to better help someone you love through learning a lesson or two for yourself. Maybe you feel stuck or hopeless or burnt out. Whatever your reason for coming to this book and making it this far, hold on to it. Look at it. What drove you to this moment?

What did you hope to gain from opening these pages? Your immediate response may be, "*I want to be less stressed.*"

Great! But why?

The forces that influence us and push us in life matter. They can change the course of our life. But you only get to be in control of your course if you are aware of what you want and what you fear, and which of these two drives are stronger.

I often like to think that we all come to a point where we overcome our fears and push through to the life we want to have. But the reality is we spend so much of our time and effort and energy on things that don't matter. Not when it really counts. Not when we look back.

If you've been as fortunate as I have to be able to talk with the people in your world who have lived a long life you will hear two things. You will hear **the moments that mattered most** to them: that first date, the feel of a loved one's embrace, the satisfaction and peace from accomplishing something they worked hard at for years to achieve. You'll even hear fond memories of that one disastrous vacation where everything that could go wrong did, or those years where they struggled and life was hard.

And you'll **hear their regrets**. The moments when fear held them back, when they wished they could travel back in time and make a different choice, or chose sooner to focus on what really matters.

This may seem like a lot. A lot of nonsense. A lot of idealism. A lot for a little book to achieve.

It is my hope that you can apply not only the skills learned, but also explore the patterns in your life that have taken you to this point to begin with. I have no desire to give you bandaids. I want to help you address the factors that led to the stress in the first place. Sometimes it may not be anything you did. Maybe you're just trying to survive one hit after another. But the way we approach any situation can impact how we come out the other end.

So ask yourself: At the end of the day what's the point of doing all of this? Why does it matter?

If you could look back on your life, what moments will stand out to you and why? Will it be the jerk who cut you off on your daily commute or the passion you have for your work? Will it be a big house or the memories you make within its walls? Will it be working so hard to escape inevitable pain and feeling stuck, or the acknowledgment that to move toward what you want most in life you will experience pain along the way? And then do it anyway because it's worth it.

There are few guarantees I can make, but one I feel comfortable making is if your immediate reaction is, *"I will do all the things that matter to me when I'm no longer stressed, when it's easier, when I'm in a better place"* then you will wait forever. Because **it is often the ways we approach (or don't approach) life that maintain the patterns of avoidance and stress.** It always seems to get worse over time even if we're spinning our wheels faster.

So again, I will ask you. What matters most to you in your

life? Who are the people you care about? What are your passions? And how do you want to carry yourself through life? How would you want the people you love or respect to describe you? Not how they do, but how would you want them to describe you?

With those questions answered, you can begin to map out a path for your life. A path where at every junction you have a choice: to move toward what matters even in the presence of pain or discomfort, or to always move away from pain at any cost. And there will be a cost. Only you can decide what you are willing to do. What you are willing to face. But with these questions answered you are in control of where your life leads.

A friend of mine, who is aspiring to incredible things, once told me that he lives his life with the intention to never regret anything. With that motto in mind, he is willing to face any obstacle, any failure, any fear because he is confident in the type of life he wants to lead. We had this conversation many years ago and it stuck with me. When you know what matters to you and you decide to chase that regardless of the pain that can come you are free.

I cannot guarantee you will meet all of your goals and with almost certainty I can say you will face fear and pain, but if it's in the service of what matters most to you it'll be worth it.

So what does this have to do with stress? How does setting boundaries with your family, saying no to your boss, or suffering through those first few weeks of starting an exercise program transform into living a life without regret, into living a life that is guided by everything you love most in this world and strive to be?

For most of us, it is a series of almost innocuous stressors that set into motion small shifts in our behavior that if looked at in slices of moments don't really seem that big of a deal. However, these stressors and the decisions we make in the face of them set in motion certain patterns of behaving that have the ability to set us far off course. Their effects are greater than the immediate experience of them.

This is how something mundane can lead to breakdowns. This is how constantly putting off what you want until your pain goes away leads to a path of isolation looking back and wondering how you let the best things in life slip away.

To break those patterns we use the tools and strategies in this book to start small. Every single decision you make, if you pay attention and are aware, can take you toward your life. You don't have to be perfect every time. In fact, many times you will pause and decide that avoidance is what you need right now. Maybe it will take a while of trial and error before you figure out how to navigate and interact with the pains in your life.

That is okay.

Keep noticing. Keep paying attention to what happens when you take a step closer to something or someone important to you. And when you move away from pain and fear and hopelessness and stress, notice. With each moment you notice you will get better at evaluating how avoiding works and whether it is worth it in the end. Continue to ask yourself, "*What is important to me in this moment?*" and follow it with, "*Am I willing to experience pain, old demons, fears for the chance at chasing the life I dream of for myself: a life without regret?*"

This will be an ongoing journey. I am glad to have walked part of it with you. I cannot guarantee a life free of pain or happy outcomes if you walk the path towards your values. Yet I do know stress will follow you where ever you go and it is my belief that if you're going to experience it anyway you might as well do what you want and learn to carry that stress with you. It's even harder than fighting it or trying to pretend it's not there. But over time that ticking of the stress time bomb becomes background noise to a life well lived.

THANK YOU!

Thank you so much for reading this book. I hope it helps you on your journey.

One of the ways this book finds it's way to people who need it is through reviews. The more reviews a book has the higher likelihood it has of coming across someone's search. If you have enjoyed this book, please consider writing a review on Amazon so it has a better chance of reaching someone who could benefit from it.

Thank you. It means a lot to me.

And if you would like any of the worksheets, downloadable mp3 files for mindfulness practices, or access to my webinar please subscribe to my mailing list at busymindreboot.com for free access to everything.

ABOUT THE AUTHOR

Dr. Jessica is a licensed psychologist, trainer, and all around self-improvement enthusiast. Originally from the States, Dr. Jessica lives in Ontario, Canada where she works in private practice and travels abroad giving trainings throughout North America.

For more books, courses, and updates:
www.busymindreboot.com

instagram.com/busymindreboot